T

Stav Poleg's poetry has appeared on both sides of the Atlantic, in *The New Yorker*, *Kenyon Review*, *Poetry London*, *Poetry Ireland Review*, *PN Review* and elsewhere. A selection of her work is featured in *New Poetries VIII* (Carcanet, 2021). Her graphic-novel installation, "Dear Penelope: Variations on an August Morning," created with artist Laura Gressani, was acquired by the Scottish National Gallery of Modern Art. Her theatre work was read at the Traverse Theatre, Edinburgh, and the Shunt Vaults, London, and most recently at Kettle's Yard gallery, Cambridge. She serves on the editorial board of *Magma Poetry* magazine and teaches for the Poetry School on a range of subjects including poetry inspired by the *Divine Comedy*, the *Odyssey* and the cinema of Fellini. She lives in Cambridge, UK.

First published in Great Britain in 2022 by
Carcanet/Northern House
Alliance House, 30 Cross Street
Manchester, M2 7AQ
www.carcanet.co.uk

A CIP catalogue record for this book is
available from the British Library.

ISBN 978 1 80017 237 1

Book design by Andrew Latimer
Printed in Great Britain by SRP Ltd, Exeter, Devon

The publisher acknowledges financial
assistance from Arts Council England.

The City

STAV POLEG

CARCANET POETRY

TABLE OF CONTENTS

C'era qualcosa di insostenibile nelle cose, nelle persone, nelle palazzine, nelle strade, che solo reinventando tutto come in un gioco diventava accettabile.

Elena Ferrante, *L'amica Geniale*

CAMERA

So the sun's sensational yellow. The river, dark iris and ultramarine. There's a girl on a train as if she's featured on-screen. Lips, bicycle red. Sunglasses, cerulean ink. Hair, Da-Vinci's flying machine. In her palm, the heart of a plum. A blue heron by the water, watching rain rain into circles, into the street. Sometimes people make a fuss over moments in the painter's life, but we know there are no moments, there are dreams and do they count? Shall we add a streetlamp? It's getting dark. The sky, kingfisher feathers. The hands, holding a torch. The heron-blue stretched over the highway in a rainstorm reservoir. Plum trees flower into smoke like in a still shot from a film noir. Yes, there are stars. Yes, front lights flicker and blossom into the night. Yes, the river is flowing and impossible. Ladies and Gentlemen, I give you. The city.

ALPINE

This morning she breathes in smoke,
watches how clouds flower

rain.
Around her, trees grow like bottles

of whisky.
The moon is a magnetic-north

feather,
shifting away

from the glass.
Now,

waiting.
The radio is on, the TV is on, words falling

like leaves on the forest-floor
snow,

buses roaming outside like big cats,
the neighbour

shouts at his girlfriend,
a door

shuts.
There is noise everywhere. Everywhere

there is silence.
Her eyes are rice-field terraces,

suspended in water
or smoke.

Outside snow is tucked under
snow-leopard

fog.
The ring

of a bell like a thunder uncurling.
She opens the door.

TOOTH

It begins with November, a moon escalating, a river asleep
and awake. The girl with the yellow hairclip
steps out of the 5 a.m. train, a cyclist—

watch out—the imprint of raindrops
on impossible sand. The day starts
with fog flowers. Restarts

with coffee, Liverpool Street, the girl reading the girl
in the French Marie-Claire, *Maigrir*
Autrement, the hiss

of espresso in London Bridge Station, the rust
on the scaffolding's spine like blue
arrows, the waiter's *everything's fine?* How you never

answer the phone.
All the way back from the Tate
I'm not crying. The Thames fires quicksilver

light, the tarmac's high fever pounds like a definite
thought—and to think I wanted to tell you a story
that began with a river and ended

with a bow. The wrath of Poseidon, the train's flashing
hours, like on-and-off sketches
of boats. At home: finish the Rimbaud, call

the dentist, it's been two years, book the Botticelli
Reimagined at the V&A, read more Sempé because you know
it works. Call the dentist.

Read it like poetry—don't expect
to understand everything—
fill in the gaps with your own
half sentences. Don't read translation
theories. Just don't
treat a language as if it's a precious
vase that could break
any second. It is a precious vase. It breaks
while we're talking—that's why we fall for it and
with it, and—listen—you have to
think for yourself but in more
than one language, and yes—life is
an exercise in freethinking, and yes—
a different language could make you
furious at first—and isn't it
strange? But so many things
can happen: the moon, a Pegasus wing
at your door, a telephone ring
(and you know who
I'm thinking), the sky making
no sense. So many things
may never. But listen—don't listen
to me. Listen to yourself. You wouldn't
believe it.

Summer solstice (first scene). A girl with a knife cuts a pear
in half. Think 'Venus Rising from the Sea' goes city
and smoke. At the bar, a man dreams a glass of champagne
like an unbalanced thought. Think 'Streetcar' goes 'Gatsby,' the scene
with the boat. She lights a cigarette as if it's made of thin glass,
he's telling a story as if it's a city uncut. Cut.

A nightmare. The girl shouts in a black-and-white dream. Cut.
There's a gallery. Think MOMA but rough. She looks at a pear
made of bronze, in a nest of cast iron and glass.
The gallery turns into a field of white roses, a white city,
is it still June? Think Fellini's dancing scene
in '8½.' One hand's filling a glass with champagne

the other offering the glass. *Champagne?*
The girl dances and dances. Think Matisse, 'The Cut-Outs.' Cut.
Close-ups: Scissors. A dancer. Another dream scene.
Think 'Last Year at Marienbad,' the moon like a pear—
the shape of a question. The actors arrive at an improvised city,
think musical setting, the sky made of turquoise-stained glass.

London. A waitress with eyes like stained glass.
Think Soho stilettos, fake mascara, cheap champagne.
The phone rings with a 'Moon River' cover. Think New York City
at the end of the line. *Can you hear me? We've met at the*—. Cut
to a mirror. Think Manet's 'A Bar at the Folies-Bergère.' Cerulean pear
made of a girl and a corset too tight. But next, it's the girl with the scene-

stealing smile. Ready? It's 'The Perfect Summer' deleted scene:
a lake, pink lemonade, a girl's wearing soft tan. Think 'The Glass
Menagerie,' anything but. Sunglasses like a Venetian mask, a spiral pear-
and-amaretto tart, she drinks too much champagne
then hides and throws up. Think 'Manhattan,' the outtakes. Cut.
Rome. A girl opens an envelope with the tip of a knife. Think 'La Città

e la Casa,' pages revealing city by city as if every city
is cut into rivers and sliced into streets down to the seeds of each scene.
The phone rings. *Don't hang up*. She hangs up. Cut.
Later, she watches how sand travels like rain inside hourglass
bulbs as if it's a low-budget film. Sound effects: rain, champagne
flute drops from a hand. Somewhere a girl wears a ring like a pear

on a knife, like the deepest of cuts. Somewhere a city
is closed and is endless, is the shape of an 8, a pear mise-en-scène
where a glass stem is held like a spine and a promise. *Champagne?*

UNTITLED FILM STILLS

(Twelve variations on that thing falling visibly)

Here, the singer-songwriter sorts out a wardrobe
of rain. In the half light, two pictures: a glass hovers
and lands on the closed-guitar case. On a shelf, the quick blue
in a contact-lens shell. A sketch of a harbour—far off—
in a simulated, extraordinary
rain. Next, football-pitch floodlights in charcoal
and rain. In this one, the trees of parachute blue, the street
in the dark. Here, a crescent—what's left
of that night. Next, the two schools of thought on the nature
of rain: a self-portrait—whether she's crying or
singing, well. Here, 'an empirical study of driving and
rain.' In this one, this is what I meant when I said
rain. A frame following a frame. She's driving to see you
and she knows you're not there.

IN THE STUDIO

I wanted to do all this

to flatten a bead to a disc—a leaf of sea
glass, to find the blue of a rose
in the quick of my wrist, to catalogue
every streetlight, each impossible rumour, the silver
of trees, to circle the city—my pulse in my palm
like a spring. Was the night open
to that possibility—the sky, an equation
of stars versus full-hearted
rain? I wanted to test how a gesture
turns into a physical land—an amplified
thought, how it changes when connected
to sound or joined to a sketch of blue
light, I wanted to watch how a lightbulb ends up
standing for light.

That night the city was unapologetically

there: a finally, fully
developed concept of streetlights and
rain. When the bridges took off
in a great-pelican flight—entrusting the river
to us—I gave names to each applicant:
the tracing-pink glass, the girl with a penchant
for imperatives, the band at The Drunk Anarchist
trying out turn-of-the-century
jazz and blue smoke. Remember, your material
is words. Was the night cerulean, cold and
misleading? Was the city that different to the one

you had left with a friend? I now understand
what I thought I couldn't: the place where
I'm confident is here.

The flight of plates

didn't happen at once or according to plan.
When the spoons lifted their wings with a cry
of miniature birds, heading north and then
south, trying out clicks of clear silver, the seashore
became endless with rain, the blue-heron wings
didn't make any sense but the rebelling sound
of the air—compressed and released like a girl
who would not play this game. I think she said dreams
matter. I think she said that's Okay to not
understand. I lifted the near-miss of a moon
with one hand. The sunset not setting I couldn't
explain. Mistakes always happen, she said. In fact, it is strange
when they don't, she concluded, brushing sea glass
and salt off my hair.

NOSTOS

When he returned—
in someone else's question—

I walked away to find the August
moon. Outside, the rain

ran through his *nostoi* stories
and never got tired

of setting the scene.
Somehow

he had managed to come back
and I thought—strange,

the way he acts at home
like a homesick expert, tries out

the nights between the kitchen
and the second floor,

surprised to find me waiting, walking,
there.

When he returned I didn't
ask how was the flight, or is it

too cold or is there anything, or anything
you need.

I walked outside to try
the bread of rain. Inside—

to make espresso with the new espresso
dust, to beg the moon

for patience,
for the way I seem

to never understand. Muse—tell me
of the man of many turns.

ATHENA BANDE DESSINÉE

Athena draws a crescent on the floor.
She picks it up, mistakes it

for a bow.
Nobody knows I'm an actress,

she says on the phone, draws back
a string, releases

an arrow. The olive-tree scene
turns to pieces. The back

of the street—a flipped glass. Time for a story,
she thinks.

*

At night she breathes out stories like smoke,
she likes playing

with matches.
She's had enough—leading heroes back into

language—
because 'hero' and 'home'—

f*ck.
Are you from The Odyssey? A journalist asks

at the pier,
as if privacy had always been shot

with a flash;
as if Western civilisation

had never been drawn on the shores of Friday-night cinema—
of heroines

walking out of their cities,
the gates

of their stories.
She stretches her arms like a question, her wings

like a restless boy.
No. It's not

me,
she says with a bow.

*

You have changed, the journalist says, knowing
she's lying.

And you—you never
knew it was me upon meeting, she says, knowing it's only

half true.
Half false—

a moon crescent—is almost enough
to begin with, she thinks,

picks up an arrow, draws back the city like curtains,
falls down to her knees.

*

You have changed, the journalist says. Coffee?
And you—

you always loved repetitions,
she says,

turning the glass into
sand.

*

So there was this man,
she says later at the after-show lecture:

'Lights! Camera! Sea!'
Everyone knew he was not going

anywhere near going home, so I had to
fold maps out of

mountains, give names
to false rivers, proof sound-simulations

of rain.
I made out of paper—a black-iris

valley,
the shade of a snowflake

on skin.
There were actors, directors, light

designers, but I'm not going to mention
Poseidon, because F*ck—

look what anger can do to a man—a god—sorry.
Did it work? Did art

installations lead the way
home? That's a lovely

question. Do you happen
to know the time? I'm looking for two bedrooms—centre

of town—
and I love how the shadow of morning collides

with the street lights
at dawn.

*

You have changed, the journalist says, knowing
she's always

been changing.
A shepherd. An eagle. A cloud.

And you—you always loved the same story, she laughs,
takes off her sandal, smashes a fly

to the wall.
There's always one way

that leads to another, she says. For us this 'another'
is home.

*

Suppose I'm shooting an arrow of fire into
a story. Suppose I'm taking it back—an uproar stretched out

to a hiss. Acrylic paint—yellow, a streetlamp—uprooted, the city unpacked
on the floor.

Suppose I'm hosting a feast out of the things I'm not
saying. An olive unhitched like a tooth.

*

No, you don't understand—she shouts
on the phone—

what I told the journalist—the one I thought
was my friend—

was half
true—that picture

of me shouting snowflakes—that
language—except

what I said about drawing—
the way it misleads us

into what matters—
a field

reduced
to a crow.

*

You have changed—
nobody

says.
A sketch

of a window, black ink, tracing
paper, the pulse

of a torch
in blue light.

*

Suppose I'm pressing my palm
into the windowpane seashore, she thinks, steering

the glass into fog.
The sky relocates night out of rainfall,

a hoop of a moon—a quick
thought. Nobody knows how I miss him,

she whispers,
holding onto a crescent

she takes for a boat.
Suppose I go out of this door I take

for a story.
We all do that. Right?

Her sandal, bright yellow. Her eye,
a grey heron.

The back of the street—
a flipped glass.

LEFTOVERS

For years I've been editing winter.
The rain, inaccurate. The sea,
acres of unwrapped water and nowhere
to find you,
even when I settled for finding you
in other people's coats
or move-abouts or late-night drunken
weather. Now I know enough
of winter to never
get it right. The season of failed forecasts,
recurring like a ritual,
as if seasons return only
to leave us
with the study of unsteadiness
and repetition.

Sometimes I throw flat stones into the water,
to hear them try the sea.
On other days
I find the pathway to your winter, like in a kitchen,
open white cupboards and
close them, open and open the fridge.

CIRCLES

Loss has a wider choice of directions
Than the other thing.
                    W.S. Merwin, 'The Nails'

Now, as the rain turns into
sketches of rain, a girl draws a circle
on the quick-yellow sand.

In the picture, the sea is another
quick second. Hours are physical
matters, thinks the man who quit smoking

two hours ago—
in the picture. Here, he doesn't fall
into his palms, he doesn't seem

absent. Throw a pebble
into the water and watch how the circles
get bigger, thinks the woman

outside the picture, watching the snow
taking hold of a city she now
calls home.

Click

Two glasses of water waiting to happen.
Two dragonflies, blue and
quick-blue.

I wouldn't mind being that kind of adventurous,
thinks the woman watching the street
holding onto the snow.

I wouldn't mind being that kind of pretty,
thinks the child watching a bee
fighting a pond. Throw a pebble into the water

and go for a walk.
In the picture, the rain never stops
or begins, the man doesn't fly

out of the streetlights, the city,
that year. In the picture—that year
never happened.

Click

A child, cutting the sea out of blue and dark
paper. A hot-air balloon in a short
animation. A telescope catches

a moon.
I wouldn't mind being that kind of lost,
thinks the tree watching a car in the rain,

thinks the pond watching the door
open and close, thinks the picture taken
again of a circle turning

into a hole,
thinks the child drawing a rainstorm
before it takes form:

a tree practicing being a tree. A sandcastle
made out of water. Throw a pebble into the picture
and watch—

CAMERA

In French: 'la caméra.' In German—
'die Kamera.' Not every word translates unexpectedly, but look
at this: *The sonnet is a monument of praise, a field of play, a chamber
of sudden change.* In the heatwave of 2003, Hyde Park
turned yellow—not of mango sorbet
but the colour of absence. I went for the blue
leaf, the turquoise-green pond against a moon, The Penguin
Book of the Sonnet. (A short film I wasn't thinking about
then: a boy running after a spinning-blue globe—the home
movie I can't watch again—it was
lost—so I'm watching it anyway, here, in the city
I landed into that June—my summer of sudden
change.) In French—'le changement.' In Italian—
'il cambiamento.' This isn't helpful, but how about
that—ice cubes break into espresso / a sound installation
of rain / a protagonist in a language I'm still trying
to learn: *Lei era così, rompeva equilibri
solo per vedere in quale altro modo
poteva ricomporli.** Trying to read
on the train: the sound of water
bottles, crisps, a man explaining to his inattentive
daughter about the human eye: 'the pupil is a hole
located at the centre of the iris.' How else
to describe this place? In French: 'l'été.' In Italian:
'l'estate.' (A city I wasn't planning
to dream into a film, a field
of play, a chamber, a chamber—
London, the heatwave of June 2018, I'm waiting for you
at the Tate's Turbine Hall—this is how
it must feel, hiking inside the heart
of a whale—before I go

and watch how Gerhard Richter figures out
John Cage—the room
you once named 'cities in the rain,' the room I never leave
without a sense of being
left.) In French: 'la maison.' In Italian:
'la casa.' I know it's not the right translation.
(Look—a heron dives into the Thames.)
So how about this one—camera.

* 'She was like that, breaking balances apart just to see how else she could reassemble them.' From 'L'amica Geniale' by Elena Ferrante

over Cinecittà?
Or was she the sea monster pulled out of the sea?
Was she the end or the beginning? Was she the map
of Italy, the city of Rome, the water
bathing Adam and Eve? Was she the nymph lamenting
non mi tormenti più, and wasn't she
awesome as the dancer backstage / the rain in the gutter / the fire? Was she
ever alone? Was she the child running barefoot

in the black-and-white storm? Was she *Une Femme*
dont les histoires ont apporté de la joie? Was she the tall silver trees,
the cars reaching the wood? Was she the boy shouting back
at the camera hook? Was she the male journalist, his father,
his friend? The three other
girls on the August-lit roof? What was she thinking
anyway? What was she drinking? What was
her name?

TRYING TO TAME THE HEROINE IN MY POEM

was supposed to be easy. Here I am, sitting
by the towering gates of this city, street,
poem, when she's suddenly skydiving

into the scene—test-driving a river
I'm still working on, showing off
her free-falling, flying, centrifugal-force

thoughts. The trees upside down
like an unsettled sketch, the rooms with no
walls—how she's making them into her place.

*

Today we study the inner-working
of dark turquoise and green—how to improvise
a much-darker summer, carry it

into the scene. For hours I'm calling
but she's busy turning the seashore
into an open-air stage, relocating the river

to the city's stage door, adding a massive, blue
moon, too many lanterns and fictional
stars. It's supposed to be dark

and I have to take her aside and explain
that today, really, she should simply be
beautiful—beautiful

is not what I've signed up for—she cries,
throwing a deepest-green bottle
into the rose-detailed

window I've been drawing
all night. You're not going anywhere—
I say, blocking her way—not now

when you've broken the glass of this
poem. I can tell she's beginning
to laugh so I turn on the stereo snow,

throw some lightning, more
clouds, as I watch how she picks up sharp
pieces of window, glass, night, how instead

of rebuilding the frame she constructs
a small tiger out of old-telephone wires, new
rumours and sound waves,

an impossible soundtrack of rain and more
rain. For the first time—I notice—
I just let her

work on her stuff. I don't mind
if I don't understand what she's up to or where
we're going from here.

*

'Antagonism for Beginners'
is the book she's been reading
today. She sits in the balcony I've carried

all night from the street
in a dream I had failed not to visit
again. She's been quiet—too quiet,

today. Look! I say—an actual dragon
has just taken off from the fold
of your book! She doesn't respond, or perhaps

it's the snow that keeps falling into
the pages she's turning, turning
them into fields of white roses, blue-fire

lakes. Are these stories or
memories? I ask, but she doesn't reply
so I turn to do other stuff: I'm drawing

a glass—half filled with water, half carrying
air. It's difficult, separating water, glass,
space. Difficult, relying on

graphite, small movements, the chances
of rain. But perhaps, difficulty
is something I care for, maybe even

admire—I say, louder, looking
at her. I'm not sure she's got it—she's deep
in her book, pretend-reading

all day. So I open the still-broken
window to the spiralling sound of an ambulance
siren, add a few airplanes

in the absence of stars,
and when none of this works, I summon
a helicopter to lower a rope ladder

into our balcony—towards
the book she holds onto and will not
let go. I think I can tell what is happening

to me—I'm running
in and out of ideas, so I settle
for this: I draw a distant

lagoon instead of the city we're in—
here's a river moon-chasing the night
in the fine-sapphire fog, here's the shape

of the sky turning round. It is so
peaceful, so utterly beautiful—I know
she'd hate every second of it,

but she doesn't react or perhaps
it's the reason she seems to dive—deeper—
into her book. So I pick up a pencil and throw it

towards her glasses—oops! Something
is happening—sure, but it's hard to see
what, hard to figure out why a small

tiger has just crossed the room, heading
towards the almost-there window, jumping
into the night.

*

I know what you're doing—
I say, pushing the river into the storage-room
dark, untangling the ladder

from the pinned helicopter that is still spinning
the scene like an on-and-off star. I know
what you're doing—I say, sending

an airplane back into the city's near-miss
of blue sky—and it's not going
to work. I'm glad—she replies, finally

closing her book—because I haven't a clue—
she continues—you're not telling me
why, suddenly, this is all about

you. *It's difficult, sketching the chances*
of rain, she misquotes, mimicking
my voice. She takes the glass I've been

drawing and drinks all the water
I've worked on for hours: how reflections form
and reform—she drinks every atom

of that. This is actually—really—quite
difficult, so I open the door and go for a run
as far as I can—out

of this poem.
Outside, it's snowing—all
morning, all of a sudden summer

has turned into winter as if for some
reason I haven't noticed the trees following
seasons, the changing of hours

into darker-green skies. I'm running
and running—for hours, trying
to match the pace of my thoughts to that

of my pulse.
Perhaps you've been busy,
missing your friend—perhaps it's been grief

you were trying to deal with—
my heroine says—suddenly
freefalling out of the poem and into

another. Perhaps you've been
busy, not knowing how to make sense
of this mess, I mean—

loss—all this time. But look,
there's a room full of lanterns and
upside-down trees and new lights

you've just added, and sure—you can always
call me to test out the river's formation
or break something

apart. She hands me the book
she's been reading not reading before
running back to her loss, I mean—

stuff. When I open it, I can see her—just
there—how she lifts a volcano, throws
it into the ocean, how she makes

a whole city disappear and appear
with the rhythm of night. For the first time
I notice how much she has changed

since she first came around.
I've underestimated you—I almost
say before changing my mind. Thanks—

she replies, throwing the poem like a ball
in the blue-solstice air, looking at me
as I struggle to catch it. I don't know

what you're doing and I haven't a clue
what I am, I say as I watch how she's lifting
the weight of the poem

with one hand, disappearing into the absence
of window, the rooms with no walls, relocating
the river, the seashore, the night turning to rain.

HOLD

That day, when the ambulance siren
left our street in suspense—

that ring of metallic-blue
light, the way it was moving in spirals

of sound, this and the way it was
snowing—as if nothing

mattered but the paper-skin
layers of sky turning into more

sky—it was then when I held onto
my notebook's primary yellow, held onto

the road's manipulations of distance
and fog, and I knew I could always

go back to that point—the functional
place of being alert like a blade of blue

glass—but that night, a quality
I'd been losing and studying was suddenly

present, and I wanted to dream into
the snow—a form of acceptance, perhaps

a reaction I had to name
confidence—that rare, inarticulate

thing that set itself free or perhaps it was
simply the seemingly sudden, new

moon—because I looked
at the road and the fog and the blue-cherry

blossom that was dreaming far off—
and I think it was then that I finally

got it—amidst the turmoil and
sounds and the changing

of weather—it was never surrealism
that was lacking discipline,

it was that—how to call it—
other thing—

that particular hour, accidental
as it always manages to seem—

the one I couldn't explain or catch out
of the water and yet started

to name and rename
and hold onto

ANOTHER CITY

A CUP OF WATER AND A ROSE

After Francisco de Zurbarán

Had a plate been shipped from Peru to Seville—
five or so weeks through the map
of an ocean—I too

would have placed a quick rose
on its silver-brim deck. At the market—
the girls are sun-dazed with harsh summer.

If it's morning—there are horses and fields
of blue wheat, there's the washing
of plates. I too would have anchored a cup

at the focal point of a picture—pitched
a room in the light of a boat, taken
my time.

*

How to draw water.
Summer brings nothing but sky and more sky—
a new moon every hour, a girl

crossing a field.
I would have rescued a stalk off my hair, waved
to a possible ship from a harbour darkening

with salt and white
seagulls. I would have stayed
for the rain.

I'M SENDING YOU A LETTER

Inside, I've put a full-size blue guitar, a slice of sea (so you could shake it in a glass over the Mediterranean coast), a saxophone I borrowed from a local busker because I know you'd like her work, all my air-miles—so you could come and visit me—a crow, crushed ice, a glass of pink Prosecco—just open carefully—mid-August Edinburgh (a bunch of slightly boozed-up actors, a box of unpredicted rain). I marked it fragile, FRAGILE, all over. Let me know if it arrives.

THE STUDY OF STARS

Back by popular demand—
the sky sliding towards

the ground.
The flippant uncertainty

of rain.
An Olympian god lifting a city

from the deep of the ocean into
the night—

we could sketch it
like that.

From the window, the pulse
of a siren. On the table—

espresso blooms
in a glass.

I walk in Rimbaud's Metropolitan
and stop by the crystal-tree

avenues. The violets, blue
and invented. The boulevards, receding

and endless—
in this place, the planets depend

on one's own apprehension:
how we manage

or don't manage
fear.

*...et si tu n'es pas trop accablé,
l'étude des astres—Le ciel.*

I go for a run in the equinox snow—
to the river and back

to the river.
What would you give

for this hour—
when you know the direction

and are utterly lost? A glass
for another? A moon

for a torch?
What I should have learned

years and two rivers
ago: how to separate darkness from

darkness,
real from unbearably

real,
popular

from demands,
mistakes

from the ones I'm not willing
to learn from.

All that time, taking this city
for granted.

All that time, crossing the Atlantic,
thinking it didn't exist.

for your absence of blue, an element—
locked, like a star. How did it happen, halfway
through the queue, that I started
to cry? There must be a trilogy
that begins with a rose
and ends with a streetlight—a blue
dot in the snow—deceptive
like water: clear and seemingly seeking
a deeper conclusion. I would never
have given you ten out of
twenty, except on that night
when the guy at the bus stop started—*hey,
what's your favourite place?* And I noticed
the rain, the way it was fractured the second
it hit the blue lights—the tour de force
start of November. New York,
it was then when I knew it had always
been people like us—who grew up in small
places—who know nothing is worse
than the clear-porcelain moon
of blue sky, who'd go for the streetlights'
reflections in quicksilver rain—any time—yes,
give me winter's exaggerated
romanticism—a bitten-pink rose
in cigarette glass. I have fallen for each
fissure of pavement, for the crowd altering
the shape of quick
seconds, for the postman holding a pink
envelope—that wonder of physically
carrying a small piece of writing
from one place to another through snow and blue

snow. New York, that I'm writing you
here, in Monmouth café off Borough street,
London—lol—
what do I know of the light falling
backwards past Brooklyn Bridge. It's early
July and the waitress feels sorry
for me—I can tell. Perhaps it's the way
I'm holding onto the purple-blue leaf
in my bracelet as if I am trying to track down
my pulse. What do I know
of the heavy sleet turning to snow
in a city I visited once, for three
nights. Here, the Thames turning inwards, the air—
heavy with summer and impossible
heat. What do I know of the dreamers
fighting a blue-upturned umbrella
next to the Guggenheim trees, of the girl
running with a yellow guitar on her back, crying
into her phone: *where? I can't hear you*—,
of the way her breath changes with each leaf
of snow, of the man at the bus stop, calling
through fast-moving sleet and blue
smoke: *you, my pal*
for the night—what are the odds
you're into the greatest
espresso? What do I know of the yellow-plum
trees encircling a crescent
that until recently never really, particularly
mattered, of the local café
where the owner has broken
her arm and her fiancée's car and her promise
to place a blue rose every morning
on the windowsill snow until
her grief passes, or at least changes

light, or at least lets her fall
asleep in the night, of the game-changing
headline across the Atlantic, declaring
her place *c'est Un Must*, of the entire
neighbourhood's extraordinary something
of a renaissance, of the pink
envelope she opens and opens and
fires like a paper-plane into
the snow. There must be
a trilogy, where three-quarters through, you
stand in a five-hour queue
with a guy who's unlocking blue smoke
under flickering lights, who is out of his
element—and sure, so are you—yet you totally
know what he means when he says he is hoping
the coffee will live up to the hype.

OOMPH

*Of course, it's unfair to expect a restaurant to single-handedly represent
the cuisine of an entire country.*
Hannah Goldfield, 'Tables for Two', *The New Yorker*, July 23, 2018

Why did the cellist storm out
to the snow—the artichoke blue like a heart
on the waiter-pink

plate, the door—like a question—suspended
and closed? Sure, the espresso soufflé
was beyond-burning

point, the rumour
concerning the river, the spoon—
was half false and half

thrilling,
but like any dream
it kept changing, and like any spoon

it kept playing with how much
it could hold. The bassist
who left the same

evening insisted
it wasn't the oomph
he was after, the country

he'd left like a note
on his ex-girlfriend's fridge,
the star stickers

flickering on his childhood-high
ceiling that no longer
exists—no,

it wasn't the sky getting
darker and brighter, the pianist
who rarely accepted different readings

of lemon meringue,
the first violinist who—all things
being equal—would smoke anything

but ended up crying
for the flamed-chocolate tart. Why
did it matter

so much? How did it bring
back the family dinners—those infinite
winters, the flawless

frittatas their mother
never managed to make
without triggering the town's fire

alarms, the sea-water
brigade, the cats chasing the rain
from the roof

of their lands,
the man at the porch, stargazing
into his glass,

the neighbours who never
insisted on keeping their word, that certain
je ne sais quoi.

ANOTHER CITY

The way you ran into the last rush-hour of the morning,
like a character in one of Sempé's city sketches,

with your coat collapsing and the wind
not helping, water-coloured by the racing cars and rain,

which wasn't even falling enough
to cause such a storm. There's a picture, or a place,

where everyone's thrown in their city's steps and hours,
walking or smoking into each other,

holding their phones, *T'es où? Allô, t'es où?*
On the corner of

Baker Street and Marylebone, I think I was
the only one not moving, holding onto my mobile, to all my

where-are-you texts and messages, so I'd look busy
and not lost.

FOUND PROUST[1]

Aussitôt la vieille maison vint comme un décor de théâtre[2]. Il me semblait
que j'étais moi-même ce dont parlait l'ouvrage: une église, un quatuor[3] …tout cela
qui prend forme et solidité[4], Napoléon III et mon grand-père[5], cet escalier
détesté[6], le clair de lune[7], le kaléidoscope de l'obscurité[8], et celle aussi
du petit coquillage[9]—la petite phrase de la sonate[10]. À cette époque j'avais l'amour
du théâtre[11]. Je voulais aussi que la tempête fût absolument vraie[12]. Chaque jour
aux Champs-Élysées[13], à Venise, à Combray[14]—un espace à quatre dimensions—
la quatrième étant celle du Temps.[15] Vous savez que je ne suis pas fishing
for compliments[16]. Que les objets de nos goûts n'ont pas en eux une valeur
absolue[17]. Les pages du livre, la rapidité de notre respiration[18], un plaisir
de l'intelligence[19]. Ce qu'il y a de gentil avec vous, c'est que vous n'êtes pas
gaie.[20] J'ai horreur des pays 'pittoresque:'[21] l'air était chaud, c'étaient les plus beaux
jours du printemps[22]. On sentait que le Bois n'était pas qu'un bois[23]. Ce fut en dormant,
dans le crépuscule d'un rêve[24]: du champ des réalisations possibles[25].

---

1 The sonnet is composed entirely of sentences from *À La Recherche du Temps Perdu:
Du Côté de Chez Swann*

2 *Combray*. The memories that come back with the effect of tasting the madeleine. Part
of a longer sentence: '…*aussitôt la vieille maison grise sur la rue, où était sa chambre, vint
comme un décor de théâtre s'appliquer au petit pavillon donnant sur le jardin…*'

3 *Combray*. The narrator on reading and falling asleep.

4 *Combray*. Back to the madeleine episode—the memories that take form.

5 *Un Amour de Swann*. Two of the characters that appear in Swann's dream.

6 *Combray*. The staircase that separates the narrator from his mother.

7 Which one? There are so many moons to choose from. Perhaps it's the one in *Un
Amour de Swann*: thinking of nothing but Odette, Swann doesn't pay attention to the
light of the moon. Or perhaps it's an earlier moon—in *Combray*—the one the narrator
looks at from the open window while waiting for his mother to come upstairs: '…*le clair
de lune, qui doublant et reculant chaque chose par l'extension devant elle de son reflet…*'

8 *Combray*. Between sleep and wakefulness.

9 *Combray*. The shape of the madeleine.

10 *Un Amour de Swann*. The *petite phrase* brings back Swann's memories of falling in love with Odette.

11 *Combray*. The narrator's self-described 'platonic love' for the theatre, at the time when he was still not allowed to go there.

12 *Noms de Pays: Le Nom*. The narrator reflects on the stormy days in the sea town of Balbec. The original sentence includes the word 'pour': *Je voulais aussi pour que la tempête fût absolument vraie…*'

13 *Noms de Pays: Le Nom*. The narrator finds himself at the Champs-Élysées instead of Florence and Venice.

14 *Combray*. The narrator spends the night contemplating on the places he visited in the past.

15 *Combray*. The narrator on the space of the church in Combray. Could this be in response to Einstein's Theory of Special Relativity?

16 *Un Amour de Swann*. Odette de Crécy talks to Mme Verdurin.

17 *Un Amour de Swann*. Swann reflects on his taste and preferences as well as on those of Odette de Crécy

18 *Combray*. The narrator's experience of being absorbed in a book.

19 *Un Amour de Swann*. One of several reasons given for Swann's spying on Odette.

20 *Un Amour de Swann*. Swann talks to Princesse des Laumes.

21 *Un Amour de Swann*. Princesse des Laumes talks to Swann.

22 *Un Amour de Swann*. Swann can't bring himself to leave Paris while Odette is there and what with the weather being so nice…

23 *Noms de Pays: Le Nom*. Years later, the narrator revisits Bois de Boulogne.

24 *Un Amour de Swann*. When Swann encounters Odette again, this time in a dream— and what a dream.

25 *Noms de Pays: Le Nom*. The narrator imagines a letter composed to him by Gilberte.

DRAWING LESSON: ROME

\- I've never been to
\- Even better. Draw

I start with velocity versus acceleration—how a city
takes off into the night, a blue motorbike
crossing a field of quick yellow—the fraction
of stars or the acres of light against
glass. It's almost November and London's a country
I can still understand. What I can't
seem to find is the place where the rain
never stops or begins—where it's constantly
there. Am I missing the point of why we take
pictures? *Click.* A kingfisher

turns into green lightnings and rain, a river
leading into a film: blue flashing circles, a siren—
far off—from the pulse of a street
in a dream, a yellow leaf spinning in a blue bicycle
wheel. On the bus I press *play*
on my pocket-quick heart—Christine & the Queens—
*Juste une paire de demi-dieux...*What I'm trying
to say—instead of going to Rome
I've been doing all sorts of things: staring
at the 4 a.m. wall, not falling asleep, running

in the snow of ten years ago—our first Edinburgh
year. *Se non si perde tempo*
non si arriva da nessuna parte (If you don't waste time
you won't get anywhere) says the physicist
Carlo Rovelli in the beginning of the quickest-blue
book I've just left on the bus. And yes, I've got to run
to the train but I do need it back and—look! A flock
of Canada geese—I wanted to tell you
about that beautiful story I was reading last week:
Up to 25 cups of coffee a day

safe for heart health, study finds. Shall we
begin? *Click.* At the gallery—
'The Artist Answers Your Questions'
No, I never thought Still Life with Coffee Maker
would become such a hit. It is strange, pushing against
the pulse of a river I can actually
get, running the moon or the thought of a moon in a telescope
sketch. All night on the train I walk in the snow
from that Edinburgh day: an envelope
floats in the air—half

open—before diving into the poplar-blue
fields. In the morning, the sea from the window, a message
from Élise: she recommends I go back
to the very first 'Osez Joséphine—'
Juste une paire de demi-dieux... or the way
Agnès Jaoui turns it into a conclusion to that end-of-summer
party in her film. There are many variations and the rain
turns into lightnings against the yellow leaves. I'm supposed to be
in Rome, I think, and all roads lead me
out of it:

between the polar coordinates of a train
that I keep boarding and my soaring caffeine intake,
I succumb to poetry as a temporal
art—a leaf under a print of a leaf, the precarious blue
of a sky turning dark. I could hold onto the storm—
how it turns into sonority—the velocity of snow against
the lightest glass—I could stay here for a while,
but I'd better catch the bus, the night, the point
of picture-taking, and find a way into a city I keep trying
to near-miss.

YOU'RE GOING TO LOVE

the third scene in my first
novel. It involves skydiving
from circling paper planes into the blue-parachute
night, and cities—expanding
from one page to another, the way I imagine words
to behave when propelled by multiple calls
of attention or the changes
in light. 'Flowers brought to life
by magnetic pendulums' is what happens
in the second draft. I'd like to think of language
the way Takis constructed his Magnetic Fields:
'Not a graphic representation of a force, but the force
itself.' I'd like to walk in this kind of city
all night—the guitar on my back like a shield
or a backpack—and you're going to love
the way my protagonist almost misses
the train into the third
draft—the nights, the rain, those open fields
of solstice stars, how she falls in love
with everyone in that colossal, high speed
summer between the fourth and seventh
drafts. There's a warm, new
moon—that work-in-progress yellow—
above the city's lights. Stand on the roof
and look into the sliding skylight—
there's a figure running down the growing-spiral
staircase all the way after an apple
that is rolling back into
the second draft. A changing
scene—a fishing village—years or seconds
later, is where the evening soars and magnifies

into the night. It's getting dark, but you can tell
it's her—the way she's running
through her fifth, sixth glass before she throws it
backwards in an arc towards the bay, the pier,
the waves that pulse quicksilver
light, and when it starts to snow, snow
heavily until she disappears, I run
across the street to catch the bus and bring her
back into another summer, city,
draft. There's a picture
of a girl, half studying an hourglass—an apple
and what's left of it—the shape, that circular
impression changing in her palms. But this is someone
else's picture. My protagonist has spent
the night behind the sixth draft's seaside curtains—
throwing up. All those lands
and possibilities, all those clear-blue
vodka shots and stars. It's only then when we begin
to understand the title: 'A Complete
Mess,' or 'What the Actual F,' which aims to turn
an abstract into a specific incident, say—
a flower, an actual
rose, a grey-blue feather initiating
a lightning storm. There's a phone ringing
in the half-lit corridor that's leading to the seventh
draft. There's a girl catching a flying, yellow
tennis ball before it flings into the eighth floor's moon
or moon-reflecting glass. There's an airplane landing
in the snow of that spring equinox,
the ninth. There's a city, half-emerging
in the rain. 'Here's why it's OK
for Taylor Swift to use literally, figuratively,' is what
I've been freefalling into between bus-stops and
drafts, newspapers,

the train. There's a girl dreaming
a green balcony overlooking that point
in the sea from the top of a nine-storey
spinning design. So perhaps it's simply a question
of balance: is she going to back-somersault
all the way into the ocean
while pouring it into her glass? You're going to love
the sound of the waves breaking into
the pages of the tenth draft. How she navigates
into the bigger, leading role
in the now-deleted chapter: 'her
father, running from one photograph
into the other—' where she studies all the pictures
he was never in. Where she tries to understand
how grief keeps spiralling into microscopic
lands. The way some summers are impossible
to catch—a girl skydiving from the rooftop
of a draft into the solstice air. *I was literally going
to break.* Today I'm going back
to Roland Barthes and 'The Death of the Author—'
how—reassuringly—it is about birth: that of
writing—that kind of land. *It is not the expression
of personality, but an escape
from personality,* wrote Eliot earlier and today
I'm trying out expression and
escape. There's a myth
of a girl who was circling a metropolis all
winter until every streetlamp took off the ground
into the icy-blue air—like small spaceships
of light. You can find them
in the eleventh draft, past the spiral staircase, highways,
apples, seaside towns. There's a story
I keep telling myself: that the protagonist
was never lost as long as she walked with a guitar

on her back. Not lost when she took
the wrong turns, the hours
of rain, not when she couldn't stop running
for over twelve drafts. All those rivers, new
silvers of smoke and small lights. All those new-forming
lands. *Not a graphic representation of a force,*
but the force itself.

The girl at the till counts to three.
There's a key on the floor, a fish flying
in a far-northern pool, a picture she blinks with the click
of a mirror. Did she work on rhetoric with you? Did she show off
her teeth? There's a walk in the park she's keen to regret. Did she
tell you? A word is always out there looking
for words. And no—she doesn't recall. What
boy?

The girl at the till lifts a feather out of her thoughts. She watches
the day turning inwards: the rain like a false assumption,
the smoke like a bee in her throat. All those acres
of lights. There's a moon playing catch
with a pond. A great bear disconnecting itself from a dot-to-dot
argument. She picks up a thought from the floor. *Is this yours?*
She asks the man playing guitar
on his phone.

JULIETTE

Where to begin?
The woman ringing the bell of a tower
was swapping the sea
for a coin. Why did she give us a fish
when we asked for
directions? Night brought in
more questions in the shape
of a taxi, a spinning
train station, an open-till-late
tapas bar—*The wrong plate.* I was
hiding behind the magnifying glass
of a tear. You were wearing a rose
like a scar. The rain featured
a firth, a city unwilling
to dress up for winter, a mast
of clear sky—a flash banner—
*This is not what it looks like
and yet*—. The bus took us back
into the city's aesthetics—
the smoke and the granite, the scales
coming off a bronze key
like the blue in a maple-leaf
cut. The storm like a proof
in the making—
this place heaving with rumours
and locks—used to be where we meant
to begin.

That I wanted to find you here—in the land of water, skyscrapers and water—past the ice-skating fields, the pink-silver trees in Westferry Circus, the crowd—always the crowd—under One Canada Square, the smokers, outside, gazing into the waters from the Heron Quay vapour of cerulean / blue / grey, the near-miss of a reindeer in neon-red snow, the ice-sculptor willows, the January moon like a high-profile prop—what was I thinking, calling and calling your name.

SITE-SPECIFIC STREETCAR

I'm thinking commedia-dell'arte city square,
no setting,   no seats,
                    but only   as a starting point,

the air is thick with nicotine,   the breath
                    of alcohol and sleeping

pills,   some locals
                entering a pub,   a few girls
            gossiping,
            but no sight of a leading lady
                because in this free variation on an anti-heroine,
                    the one I've got in mind

is you—and if you're
quick enough   you'd catch
                            the train   into the smoke
                    of Stella-for-star street corner, the pulse
        of passing trams, the speed
                        of empty bottles
                    breaking at the

ground.
Now look for her.
Note: bring a suitcase, heavy
        with clothes you can't afford,   stay away

            from streetlamps,   silence,
                    fill in quiet spaces with words   and

worries,   hang on to whisky, skilled
                    flirtations,   hand mirrors,

        the kindness of stories, then—
                                    go

                and find her—

let them go.

I'M BACK IN THE RECORDING STUDIO

I'm back in the recording studio—
testing salt against

choice.
On your left-hand side—a city grows out

of a river. On your right-hand side—
I thought

we were going home but instead
there are trees of blue-green, a paper-boat

map. I'm back
in the recording studio—testing smoke

against glass.
If you look back—my sister

waving her hand. A carousel spinning
into an ammonite shell.

Nobody's shouting *Where are you going?*
It's not that.

*

Now that you dive into three different languages, you're—
the mouth of a river / a ship

of three masts / the gorgons running in six
directions. Backward and forward and

backward.
I thought we were going home—but instead we're going

home. I'm here
at the recording studio—testing dream

against light.
On your right-hand side—a door. On your left-hand side—

a shout. Now that you swear
in multiple

tongues!
Now that you're back.

Nobody's saying *Why are you crying?*
It's not that.

FLOATING ISLANDS

I

A girl holds a Galapagos
in her hands. A tortoise, a black feather, a leaf.

On a table, a glass carries the Pacific
and a yellow fish.

Up on the ceiling, a figure is curled in a hoop,
the archipelago moon.

The stage is a lake / a kingfisher nest / an aquarium neon-green.

You choose.

By the water, a silver heron.
            The slowest / fastest of birds.

Take 1.   Take 2.   Take 3.
                              Don't look.

II

In the blink of an eye, an evening.
In the blink of an evening -

                    spotlight -

            a blue egg on the floor.

The stage is a nest / a plate / cities of water.

The girl holds the egg by her ear, like a shell.

[Sound effects:
    a baby tortoise hatches from an egg / an ambulance siren.
                                             Your take.]

What broke once is already broken.
It won't break again.

The girl lets go of the egg.
              It floats in the air.

Instead of a moon.

III

Instead of a moon.
In her palm a starfish / a seahorse / an ammonite.

                              Close-up: a curled stone.

In the background, three parallel screens:

1. A horse running in a still shot.

2. A plum, tight, like a fist in a cube of ice.

3. The sun: resetting / resetting / resetting. The stars, glasses
   of red wine.

By the water, the heron watches the stones turn to hours,

                                   hours to stones,

    a movement into a fossil,

               a photograph.

Take 1.   It's yours.   Take 2.   It's gone.

                                    Don't lose it.

                                  Hold on

                         tight.

IV

On the stage: a room-sized Camera Obscura.
The audience gets in.

                Instead of a moon, a hole.

On the opposite screen: a girl, upside-down,
eating a plum.

A man reads her a story
from the end to the beginning.
    The book is open over their heads,

                  like a roof.

Once upon a time there was a girl.

        The man closes down the book.

V
Instead of a moon: lights project from a spinning mirror-ball.

On a table: glasses, bottles, snacks.

Don't forget, you shouldn't drink

on an empty stomach.

[Sound effects:
        clinking glasses /
                        apple bite /
                                nervous laughter /
        hands reaching for crisps /

beer can opening / champagne opening / red wine

                poured into a glass /
                                another glass   /

        another glass /   another

                glass.]   Your choice

                                of music.

VI
Wherever it is, this is not home.

[Sound effects: Canadian geese migration /

                                Russian city /

                Cowboy theme]

Instead of a moon, a map.

[Sound effects: Ocean waves /

                    Parisian boulevard, evening /

                        Shanghai seafront, day /

            Slow-motion: a baby tortoise
            hatches from an egg   /

                  A man shouts: *Taxi! Taxi!*]

Now hold on to your memory like to Minotaur horns.

        The stage is a city / a taxi / the view from a train.
                                      Your call.

VII
Close-up: an old-style telephone, red.

The girl puts the phone on her lap.
She dials little arches.
                    1   2   3
                                  Hangs up.

She dials three almost-circles.

                    9   9   9

VIII

A girl carries an egg as big as the moon.

Soon a tortoise will hatch from the moon like a shout /
a labyrinth out of a Minotaur /
an ammonite uncurled from its stone.

The girl untangles the moon.

[Crowd applause]

It is no longer round like a fossil, it is flat like a river, it is still like rain.
A photograph.

You don't need to hold a picture in your palm
to know it's not there.

You don't need to hold a picture in your palm
to know it is there.

The stage is a labyrinth / someone else's / your home.

In the background two parallel screens show two pictures:

1. A girl pushing a pram.   2. A floating island.

RAIN

When the plate diagonally
fell, like a hoop or a ring—the spin

of a coin—
I had to adjust

my yellow hairclip, the swing
of a door, the children test-driving small hours

of rain.
How to measure

the distance from here to twelve
years ago. A treehouse-blue

leaf,
a thought like a shoot

from the stem of a dream.
The reason I made the transition from acting

to directing—said the girl in the film—
was because it was raining

all June.
The reason I fell asleep reading—I said

to myself—was because I was finally not looking
for you.

AFTER-PARTY

ET TU?

*Tu as dit sérieusement, sans distance, sans un soupçon d'ironie, le mot
'déconstruction,' toi, mon ami.*

Yasmina Reza, 'Art'

Look closer, here is the water
we dream. Your eye for a comic-strip

ocean, my weakness
for rain-following

streets. Look
closer—I'm always the writer

test driving the sky with no
moon—a yellow plum

by the fire, a boy
checking himself out

in a curved-mirror
spoon. So tonight, let me drive you

into my own, compositional
weather—shall we

balance a glass
on the unstable dream

of a table?
Are you with me—

my friend?
Have you got the wrong

message? It happened
to me a few seconds

ago, and last week
during 'Art' of all plays—of all

places—
when I had to look

for the things we call
keys. Language is all we are

left with—
I thought, holding on tight

to the missing back
of my seat.

AFTER-PARTY

Yes, there was the abundance of nightfall—
the sky with a parachute scar,
the spoon clinking

on glass.
But no one could trace, like a hymn,
the blue-vanishing

trail of an apple-throw
arc. Things like this
happen—

a hula-hoop pivoting
beauty, a wonder thrown
like a firework into

the crowd.
Some say it was only
an arrow, meaning—

an error.
Others swear they could hunt down
the deepest

of sighs.
That the transformation
from an apple into

a question
was inevitable—
that the answer was no more

than a boy
offsetting fire with sci-fi
animation—I mean—what

would you choose?
The possession of Europe and
Asia / the greatest of warriors' rivers

and tongues—the green in their night-vision
maps / a doorbell and how it rings
night.

SATURDAY

And on the seventh day I said
F*ck—I totally left out

Language.
The shops

were closed, I was planning
to do—or rather enjoy—nothing, but how exhausting

it was not checking
my phone?

Very. Very

demanding.
All night, bruised flowers

turned into flying
machines. Sh*t—did I really not mention

Dreams?
What sort of a manifesto

have I been testing out
all week? At sunrise—language

was buzzing like an impossible

bee—think, think—
did I simply not

notice?
Let me get it straight—I didn't forget

to create Language or
Dreams, and yet somehow, they were

already there—before water
turned into water, before

birds realised into
wings. Was that the thing called—

Chaos? By whom?

A friend advised to look into
Plato—The Idea of River

preceding an actual River.
(Logics. Deduction. The changing

of mind. No—I haven't forgotten
to create them,

Damn.) Besides, I can play
this game too—

the Idea of Apple preceded
the fall. The Idea of Hope preceded

the espresso to-go. Was I more than aware
language was simply

a tool with which I broke nights
into sunsets?

Hell, yes.

Let there be Light
a fine example

of how syntax drives
action—a personal high

as writer-director—an empirical
study in minimalism and

Whoa! Bang!

and what a showstopper
in the original script (f*ck—

Translation!) But was language really
there before everything

else?
Let there be years before actual

Light?
The Idea of Camera

preceded projector, popcorn,
late-cinema

night.
The Idea of Popcorn preceded—

Popcorn?
Am I getting this right?

I'm looking into Einstein's theory
of time—

that time is not linear—
that it is us who are moving, not

time, us who are crossing physical fields
of gravity and light—

I know—F*ck—

and that—wait for it—
once we sort out the logistics of starships, light,

speed—we could travel
to the future and

back to the present (the present
that doesn't exist because time is not

linear) not only
in theory. Theory:

how chaos materialized into weekdays and
hours, sunsets and stars, lions,

trees, hippos.
Was my work really that

LITERAL?

(Well, I don't know anymore. Is traveling back to no present literal?)

The idea that the creation
of a literal world has knocked me for six

is more than insulting. On the seventh day
I didn't need rest, I needed

a drink.

Time plus Space equals Creation preceded

'A Room of One's Own.'

On the seventh day I held onto a room with no windows or
walls—a room built of

sound.
In the beginning was the Word. How beautiful

in English—*Word* so similar
to *World*. Are we really

going to throw in Wittgenstein
at this point?

The meaning of the world must lie outside the world

Because traveling back to it—I still don't know
which came first. What I do know

is this: language is the one thing
I keep thinking I've finally

got.
And since you're impatient—and as far as I can tell—

the egg.

(Does that transform me into a believer
in potential—in what's left unsaid—

rather than the fallout
of constant, constant

noise?
Perhaps,

but talk to me again
on Monday—my mind

inclines to ping-pong differently
on my way to work.)

TWO PICTURES OF A ROSE IN THE DARK

Il film si scrive con la luce
Fellini, *Fare un Film*

In the beginning there was the film—the night running a story
of rain: the girl holding her heart like a lightbulb, a yellow rose
as an opening scene. In the fog-turning distance, the harbour—a camera
overlooking the sea. Maybe I shouldn't be running
from Wittgenstein to Fellini like this: two pictures of a rose in the dark,
two books wrestling their wings, but look how I'm turning the light

to the rain-trembling street: *I have said it many times: in cinema, light
is ideology, feeling, colour, depth, atmosphere, story.*
I've pressed play and replay on the flowering dark
of this evening. The rain, this warm soundtrack. The moon, a blue rose
on the city's backstage. A note for the night: the stage is a motor running
language as play. In the beginning there was the camera—

a chamber of air. The night leading out of my camera
has taken me here: *for me, in fact, cinema is image, and light
is its fundamental factor.* In the beginning there was motion, running
into and out of a dream. I carry a box with a streetlamp, a story
I'm still making up: a rose starts and restarts like an engine, a rose
like a code taking form in the light. The snow, a dark

rumour doubling as play. In the beginning there was Dylan's *Not Dark
Yet*, a song in the distance, a feather midair, the click of a camera
capturing rain. Grief is the holding of an invisible rose
in the icy-blue air. Writing is running. *The film is written with light.*
Language is motion. Theatre, action. The story
is this: when I said reading Wittgenstein, I meant running

in Wittgenstein. A field is always a question of running
in every direction, a stage taking off. Two pictures of a rose in the dark—
two chambers of play. *The visual room seemed like a discovery,* a story
Fellini would lift with one hand, turning the crane of the camera
to the point where *a room can be empty and yet flooded with light*—
a projector, a screen, in the beginning there was the rose—

a gray flash in the dark. The image as opposed to the idea of a rose—
shall we press play? *It's too hot to sleep and time is running
away,* a song standing in for the long distance of light,
the dark turning darker was only the beginning—the safe, crowded dark
of a theatre night. *The story is nothing.* I'm raising my camera
up in the air like a glass. I'm not at all drunk. *There is no story*—

in the beginning there was a word firing light: *And if I say 'A rose
is red in the dark too', you virtually see this red,* a non-story running
on loop in the dark, the start in that heart I call camera.

Wittgenstein, *Philosophical Investigations,* §515
Two pictures of a rose in the dark. One is quite black; for the rose is not visible. In the
other, it is painted in full detail and surrounded by black. Is one of them right, the other
wrong? Don't we talk of a white rose in the dark and of a red rose in the dark? And don't
we nevertheless say that they can't be distinguished in the dark?

I'M LETTING VELÁZQUEZ

come up with the questions.
Does the absence of blue

resonate with the sound of imminent
rain? Is the extraordinary

yellow a tad too
rebellious for the sole illustration

of yolk as a symbol
of how easy it is—to draw

one's attention, to mistake
every circular shape for the chance

of a moon?
Things are holding together

quite well and are going
to break any

second—I reckon—but I'm letting
Velázquez come to terms

with the non-accidental theatrical
darkness around the impeccable

setting of spotlights—
the two central figures, the knife turning

the plate into a compass,
the spoon

almost touching the burning-clay pan,
the circle-in-circle

of the brass vessel, just
leaning under the boiling-oil centre

of drama and
light. Here's the palm

holding an egg
as if holding the shaping in progress

of a non-elegant
thought. Here's the boy

carrying what must be
the heaviest

moon but I know Velázquez
would say I'm going

too far.
He'd say I forgot

to give the two characters 'space—' let them
be there and

not there.
Each to their own

world of intentions and unanswered
calls,

each to their own constellations
of arbitrary objects floating

from one wall to another like an empirical
study in darkness and

play.
If you tell me

a story—he'd say—
how the glass bottle goes

with the way he's avoiding
her eyes,

or how the red terracotta
brings the light into

action until everything falls
into places—I'm

out.
So I'm letting the sounds

own the space
for a while: the wine poured into

a goblet, the door opened and
closed like a possible

action on hold.
Then he comes back, puts his hat

on the table.
No, he says, only

kidding. It's seriously raining
out there.

_____

After Velázquez, *Old Woman Cooking Eggs*

VENUS RISING FROM THE SEA

I'm a pivoting needle. I'm a circle
of constant longitude. I'm the Tropic of Capricorn / the plane of the Earth's orbit / the angle
between the ecliptic and the equatorial plane. You might say I'm the inclination
of the ecliptic, denoted by i in the figure,

but I don't think I'd care. I'm the direction along the earth's surface
towards the North Pole, I'm the compass / magnetic north / the grid lines
on a map projection. Your call. I'm 'a systematic

transformation of the latitudes and longitudes of locations on the surface of a sphere
or an ellipsoid into locations on a plane'. I'm the subject
of pure mathematical fields. I'm differential geometry / projective geometry. I'm hungry
like hell. What else

do you want me to say? I'm 'the two imaginary points
in the sky where the Earth's axis of rotation, indefinitely extended, intersects
the celestial sphere.'

BIRTH

Again I was dreaming, but it wasn't just me. There were all the creatures, incognito,
the sky and sea unseparated, and the skilfully miscast protagonists—running

towards or away from each other. You ask who I was? I wasn't
him, or her, or the one who tricked her into it—using consonants and

vowels. And even though it was my dream, I wasn't
the one turning the world—or whatever it was—

upon them, saying: if this is what you truly wish for—you may as well
match it with words.

I was the apple. The wrong and right, the bad and good, the all rounded
world-in-a-palm-of-your-hand—someone's hand. I can't recall

who held me first, or second, to find out I was all-rounded, but—God—
miles away from complete. To fall

with nothing but blood-soaked skin, high-pitched and hungry, pulled and pushed and trying
to curl as round as I'd known, until I completely

forgot—was that according to the plan? Or was there a plan? Or an apple? No one said
it was ever an apple, or that if it was—it was

falling, heavy with knowledge, into so many shaken arms
and hands.

WHAT COUNTRY, FRIENDS, IS THIS?

Perhaps you've emerged from the shipwreck of night
with a new understanding of loss. Five minutes
on the shore of this country was surely
enough to look for a stage, for the nearest
café. Enter: Viola, a captain,
sailors. Perhaps—the brass-pendulum
moon, the paper-plane mountains were too much
to take in, the new leading lady who—spoiler alert—
was trading tequilas instead of a dream. Perhaps the machine
wasn't working—perhaps
you were left with a sketch of a coin. But that night
you woke up with no inclination for testing your comedy
skills, for giving a name to a country you couldn't
explain or quick-dream. *This is Illyria.*

Come October, it was *What to expect: the first
year,* Sue Gerhardt's *Why love matters,* which I LOVED
and thought should be compulsory or handed out
for free, and *How not to f*** them up,* which was kind of
reassuring. April, it was back to
Joseph Heller's *Picture this,* because I had to. Closed
and shifting in my skinny bag, I didn't have to
open it. Just to know it was there. August, September, another
October. On my desk I've got *Into the deep street:
seven modern French poets,* Muldoon's *Plan B,*
Boccaccio's *Decameron.* For months I've been reading
none of them. The other day—
I put them on the unvacuumed floor, one on top
of the other, like an unbalanced bust or a worn-out torso,
the way things look after a rather wakeful night. A sort-of nest.
I pressed the weight of my head into the covers
for an uninterrupted doze or thought
or a few-seconds of I'm not even sure what.
What I'd been before, perhaps.

ALMOST FORGOT

– I've lost *London in a Day*.

– How did it happen?

– I can't remember where I put it.

– London?

– I looked everywhere.

– From what I've heard it's not a small city.

– No.

– So maybe it lost you.

SNOW

Drawing lesson one.
An apple. A plum.

All afternoon—the yellow mountain,
the kingfisher river—
a rumour.

Drawing lesson two.
A maple leaf. Paper cuts. Use only
blue.

Did I tell you about the driving test?
The teacher was scared.
It was the radio.

Drawing lesson three.
Poplar tree.

All afternoon—the hula-hoop
laughter. The black-iris
dress.

I'm reading a story about a girl.
It begins in the first chapter. It ends
in the first chapter.

Drawing lesson four.
Not this self-portrait. That
door.

For next time—'Normalization.'
Reading list: Rhinocéros.
BYOB.

Did I mention people buying colouring books?

All afternoon—from Liverpool Street Station
to Whitechapel Gallery—
the rain.

Drawing lesson five. Coffee?
Kentridge—'7 Fragments for Georges Méliès'

Drawing lesson six. Proportion—
the swirl of a glass, the pulse
in your hand.

Did I tell you I tried to call? I'm trying to call you
every day.

Drawing lesson seven. Describe to an outsider:
'The Peaceful Countryside'

All afternoon—that blackbird. That robin. That oak.

Drawing lesson eight.
'Knowledge versus Information'
Don't use words.

For next time—phones, sunglasses. Anything
but keys.

Did I mention the moon?

All afternoon—
Agnès Jaoui y el Quintet Oficial:
'Cuando me Faltas tú'

Drawing lesson nine.
I said—bring something you keep losing.
Why have you brought your sister?

All afternoon—King's Cross St. Pancras—
Le Pain Quotidien—

I'm reading a story about a girl.

Drawing lesson ten.
Espresso. An ice cube. You have to be quick.

Did I tell you I passed the test?

Drawing lesson eleven.
From London Bridge Station to Southbank.
The Thames.

All afternoon—Tate's Turbine Hall—
'The emptiness of the volume, the void
itself.'

Drawing lesson twelve.
Home.

We've covered watercolours, proportion, driving
techniques.

Drawing lesson thirteen.
It was evening all afternoon.
It was snowing
And it was going to snow.

Did I tell you I failed?

All afternoon—I've been drawing and
drawing and trying
to draw.

BOY

The most unlikely fish,
swimming upright like a street-lamp

in an ocean.
I'd love to say

when I first learned you were a seahorse
everything

                              fell into place.
How you'd been curled into the circles

of your spine,
breathing bubbles into your paper-cut

slow skin.
I'd love to say I've always understood

the hesitation
                    of your water-pace,

your cellophane-blue fins
          that could be wings,

or once were wings,
          the most unlikely Pegasus.

Once upon a time
there was a seahorse, a yellow seahorse,

a little lemon bubble
like a curl of light and rain.

But now that my palm is as flat
as the ocean—

I'll follow
your footprints

instead.

POOL

That day—when it all turned as clear as a shout—
your eyes of fishing villages—
your discus-throw

sigh.
We walked through the breaker of day, wearing smoke
and green sky, a porcelain

moon for a scarf. In the distance, a figure
kept wrestling with an upturned umbrella—a flowering
kite.

THE MORNING I WAKE UP IN TRACEY EMIN'S

Bed, I go back
to sleep. I sleep
into

the white
Caravaggio-like
movement

of sheets—my own
skin. The air
is gum-heavy

like eyelids,
the fields of conceptual
fever

are thrown on a mat—
two bottles of vodka,
blue

knickers, some ceilings
of vinyl-red
light, some ever-green

yellow
of pills—or is it
my headache or what

I have come to believe
of myself
for this

morning? The morning
I'm still in my bed
for three

mornings I shift out
of the sheets where she
once woke up into

the chaos
of daylight baroque—
thinking, this bed can never

define me. This
moment—this just-about
monument—this is

not me.
What if I go and just
leave it—the suitcase

heart-tight like a fist,
what if I leave it—
like this.

DIONYSIAN HANGOVER

I.

For what it's worth there's no moon left
from last night's street-stargazing
but we could fix something
tonight—press our dark sight into
the glass, manage our thoughts
in night-water.

Let's shift some wine into water, turn
the floor into a paddling pool—our living
room into a long night. Come, lie next to me,
let's hold our own Symposium.

II.

The night is long as a foreign language,
the guests are piling up their plates, and we're guests
here too—tonight,

where every glass is filled with last night's
drunken moon and makeshift

light. We start with Eros.
As if there would be any other way to start.

III.

But there are all these stories. How good we are with stories—
the half male-female bodies,

the lost equivalent
of lust.

I like this one because it makes me think of wooden toys,
of a headless something,

that even when you glue it back together
it moves and cracks, and falling still—and still,

I'm not convinced that this is it—
the way we've ended up with a half-shaped

something of a hole we may call
heart.

IV.

The flute-girl went away, the guests
are following her steps behind the ice-glazed window glass.

It's getting late. Let's gather all of our Socrates
of street-less stars—

the ones who stay awake like torches,
who even with their shoes on walk barefoot

on the icy road outside. My dear other, lover, holder
of my night-shift heart—

let's drink as if there's a Dionysian winter shaken in our glass,
until there's nothing shaken,

and winter is not winter—it is the moon's deep breath
behind the thing we sometimes think

is glass.

V.

If love is not beautiful but is the desire of beauty
If love is not wise but is the lover of wisdom
If love's lying in doorways, by roads, inside our rented-flat streets

If love dies and shoots into life and shoots into life
If love's a field and a hunter, a hunter
and a deer, a hunter and a deer—

ORACLE

We knock on her rib-cage of a house. We've brought
questions. She turns

the light off—the dark moon of sheer
curtains. She won't let us in, so we wait like a station, watch

the street flow—our great ship.
In a different city—

a 'Tête de Taureau' is always assembled
from a bicycle seat, handlebars,

the slow backdrop
of smoke.

So I try to remember—her gaze is a bull
found in objects.

We go to the backyard, pick up blue stones. The rain happens
like names.

The bartender welcomes us in—he gives us advice in the shape
of a glass. But we know

why we're here.
On good days—her voice is a wall-to-wall

cocktail bar in Havana—
her head shaking blue locks like the cores

of great fires. What I'm trying
to say—

today it seems quiet.
(Was it you who said nothing was invented from scratch—only

language?)
On good days we come to the party, don't look

for full answers, find
our way out.

So I've got to believe—somewhere a goat-leap is always declared
out of metal debris,

two flower jugs, the great leaf
of a palm.

It's a choice—isn't it? How
to cope.

The bartender stands in our way with a rum-heavy spin
on his thoughts.

If you choose to leave with nothing—he says—
try the house Mojito first.

He stares from the once-ubiquitous turquoise of eyes
into mine.

What is your forte? He asks when he fastens the glass
in my palms, opens

the door.
I thought it was me who was bringing the questions, I say.

I thought I was giving the answer, he says, points
to the lock.

Leaving—I say—*is nobody's forte.*
On bad days I manage him

better.
Today he's on form.

And neither is staying, or winter. He says, handing over
my coat.

IT IS IN LANGUAGE THAT AN EXPECTATION

Perhaps you wanted to test out a story
so you went to the balcony and constructed an airplane
out of telephone wires, a small fire, a sketch of a city
you wanted to fly as a high-altitude kite in the unsettled
weather, so you turned it into an engine, a poem
made of paper-plane wings. There are so many countries
that lead away from your balcony, a tennis ball flowering, spinning
away from the quick of your fist towards a distant-blue
circle, your pulse like a risk-taking rumour
in the long-summer evening you play on-repeat—
the street in the mirror, the moon taking shape in the room
of your script, and outside—like a study in streetlights
and rain—the city you live in and still can't afford
after so many years. But perhaps that particular 'so many
years—' if anything, gave you this small insight
to hold onto, try and release: that your own
concept of time links to that

of suspense. Somewhere, a probability—
high as the gate of a story—the one you mistake
for a place—begins to take shape, the throw of a ball
like a long-distance question, your own misconception
expanding, echoing a city you leave
and keep coming back to as if in a dream, except
this time you know you're running this dream: the balcony
takes off like a light-flying machine, the moon pulling the script
of your street as short film, the night ringing the citadel sky
like a copper-blue bell in a country you're still trying
to get, your hand raising a glass to the first
day of spring as if you have always held onto nothing
but this—the glass an exception—*that an expectation*—

a yellow ball spiralling towards an improvised
land—*and its fulfilment*—the fall or the poem you're carrying
as if you were trying to catch it or give it a name—
make contact.

Wittgenstein, *Philosophical Investigations,* §445
It is in language that an expectation and its fulfilment make contact.

Camera
The first quote in the poem is taken from Phillis Levin, *The Penguin Book of the Sonnet*, (Penguin Books, 2001), p xxxvii. The translation for the second quote is mine.

Two pictures of a rose in the dark
In addition to the title, all other quotes in the poem are taken from the following sources: Fellini, *Fare un Film*, X (Einaudi, 2015); An interview with Fellini in *The New Yorker*, October 30, 1965; Dylan's *Not Dark Yet*, Wittgenstein, *Philosophical Investigations*, 4th ed., trans. G.E.M Anscombe, P.M.S. Hacker and Joachim Schulte (Blackwell Publishing, 2009), §514, §400, and §673; and the preface: 'For it compels us to travel criss-cross in every direction over a wide field of thought.'

Venus Rising from the Sea
The quotes in this poem are taken from the sections on Map Projections and Celestial Pole in Wikipedia.

Snow
The line 'The emptiness of the volume, the void itself' is taken from: Sam Jacob, 'Scale and Expansion: The Void at the Heart of the Culture Palace,' *Art Review: Tate Modern, Nought to Sixteen, a History*, May 2016.

ACKNOWLEDGMENTS

Thank you to the following poets for reading and responding to the manuscript and for your insight, friendship and generosity upon which I've relied when wrestling with individual poems at different stages and directions: to Kaddy Benyon, the late Clare Crossman, Lucy Hamilton, Lisa Kelly, Jane Monson, Haris Psarras, Lucy Sheerman, Rosie Shepperd, Liane Strauss and JL Williams.

Thank you to John McAuliffe and Michael Schmidt, for reading my work with such care and attention and for taking my poems on this beautiful road trip, from the pages of *PN Review* via the wonder that is *New Poetries VIII* and towards *The City*.

Thank you to Laura Arena, Élise Béraud, Ioana L. Campean, Imbisaat Geti, Emmi Hartikainen, Elisabeth Klaar, Inbal Leitner and Mari Valli, for being here—Edinburgh, Cambridge, London—walking this multilingual island together.

*

My thanks to the editors of the magazines and publications in which the following poems first appeared:

- 'After-Party' and 'The City' were published in *The New Yorker*
- 'Alpine,' 'Oomph' and 'The River' were published in *Poetry London*
- 'Another city' was published in *Poetry Wales*
- 'Are you there?' was published in *Kenyon Review*
- 'Birth' and 'I'm back in the recording studio' were published in *The Rialto*

- 'Boy' and 'Dionysian Hangover' were published in *Gutter (New Scottish Writing)*
- 'Camera,' 'I'm letting Velázquez' and 'New York, I've fallen' were published in *PN Review*
- 'Et Tu?' and 'Listen, you have to read in a foreign language' were published in *Poetry Ireland Review*
- 'Floating Islands' was published in *The Moth*
- 'Leftovers' was published in *South Bank Poetry*
- 'Nostos' was published in *Brand Literary magazine*
- 'Rain' was published in *Bath Magg*
- 'Reading list, *or* What was I thinking' was published in *Magma Poetry*
- 'Site-specific Streetcar' was published in *New Welsh Review*
- 'Snow' and 'You're going to love' were published in *Poetry Birmingham*

*

- 'In the Studio' is featured as part of *Write Where We Are Now* project, Manchester Writing School website, ed. Carol Ann Duffy, July 2020
- 'Athena Bande Dessinée' and 'Floating Islands' were commended for the *Ballymaloe International Poetry Prize*, 2017.
- 'Floating Island' was performed by actor Florence Brady as part of the Polyphonic Poetry Festival at *Kettle's Yard* gallery, Cambridge, UK, June, 2018
- 'Alpine' was featured on *Poetry Daily*, October 2016.
- 'I'm sending you a letter' is published in *'A Year of Scottish Poems,'* (Pan Macmillan, 2019)
- 'I'm letting Velázquez' film poem, edited and produced by Pixel Assist, is showcased on the *National Galleries Scotland* website: https://www.nationalgalleries.org/art-and-artists/features/i'm-letting-velázquez-film-poem-stav-poleg

*

A number of these poems are included in *Lights, Camera,* (Eyewear Pamphlets, 2017) and *New Poetries VIII* (Carcanet, 2021).

*